I0159132

LIGHTS SHADOW

LIGHTS SHADOW

Dayshawn Robinson

RESOURCE *Publications* · Eugene, Oregon

LIGHTS SHADOW

Copyright © 2025 Dayshawn Robinson. All rights reserved. Except for brief quotations in critical publications or reviews, no part of this book may be reproduced in any manner without prior written permission from the publisher. Write: Permissions, Wipf and Stock Publishers, 199 W. 8th Ave., Suite 3, Eugene, OR 97401.

Resource Publications
An Imprint of Wipf and Stock Publishers
199 W. 8th Ave., Suite 3
Eugene, OR 97401

www.wipfandstock.com

PAPERBACK ISBN: 979-8-3852-3442-4
HARDCOVER ISBN: 979-8-3852-3443-1
EBOOK ISBN: 979-8-3852-3444-8

01/28/25

Contents

A PEER INTO THE SHADOW

Let's peer into the abyss, Will you continue, or Will you falter? It's the way of life peering into the shadow. Means accepting the failures and looking at others around us who have similar experiences or have different experiences. Those ahead and those behind an all inclusive, but yet written by one And all interpreted, yet written by one when you peer into the shadow, I want you to understand, when you look into the reflection of your shadow It looks back at you back at others around you read carefully and understand that this is not just about disparity, but a sense or calling to those who are with you and those who are not. You may not understand now. But read carefully and find out. Will you peer into the shadow.

WATER'S REFLECTIVE PAST

Hand reached out
Never grasping the droplets falling about
Hopes, dreams leaking off the body
Staring into the reflection that has become sodden
Never achieved but ever does it fall
Those hopes and dreams became nothing at all
Given up sinking farther
Life gets harder
Hand reached out creating one's ocean
Drowning in a soft smooth motion
Reflections fade become dark
Until the last drop sinks dampening the spark
Looking down into that watery abyss
Every future was dismissed
Closed heart and drowning soul Finally released into that deep
aqua bowl

HOLLOW WALKER

Emotion I care not
Say and do whatever I want
Sealed heart closed mind
Prance about with others not in mind
Sweet smell of freedom what I feel
Being freed from connections
Everlasting Elation
Actions never sanctioned Evil what I'm called
Speak my mind is all Nothing inside
Never will be
Dark and shadow sober
Hollow Walker please takeover

FRACTURED EYES

See but do not hear
Speak and you disappear
Walk but not far
From truth you will be barred
Head down don't breakout
If you do others will shout
Go wherever you like
But do not speak in spite
Concept of "you" does not exist
Only the collection will not be dismissed
Shadow's grasps take your senses
We will make you senseless
Let go of love and passion
But let sin's shadow give you those rations
Walk with head tall to your demise
Until you can't see with those fractured Eyes

SILENT SUFFERING

Open mouth but no words
Reaching out touching nothing
Can't grasp my earns
Walking endlessly, with no goal in mind
Life has no meaning
Fate worse than death itself
Actions erase themselves
Time spent is time lost
Even it has no mercy at all
Glass spilled and done
As my heart sinks to the bottom of the ocean
Without the light, I covered by shade
Continue Silent suffering

THE MAN WHO WROUGHT

Up rose the storm in the darkness
A man came walking shrouded like a carcass
Struggling to walk the man fought
Up rose the storm
The winds pushing him back
Making him stumble causing his feet to lack
For in the darkness, he could not see
Yet he still pushed walking endlessly
Up rose the storm
Rain beating on his head
They felt like giant boulders or lead
Even though getting terrible scars
The man never dropped his guard
Farther ahead the man could see
Fighting forward the light he's been trying to reach
Up rose the storm
It beat on him even harder
Slowly the storm making him martyr
Closer and closer he got
More the storm brought
Up rose the storm
Man became worn
He reached out his to touch the light
Until he fell accepting his plight
Fell into darkness with his hand reaching out
Slightly close to the light he sought out

Others came into the darkness and storm
But all failed to brave and were mourned
All had fell short of the man who was close
Being taken by darkness at the beginning
With only one factor in common
All reached out their hands shrouded in darkness
To the one ahead who almost touched light
Though many more come they forget those who lay
Especially the one who got so close and sought
They forget The Man Who Wrought

ROOTED INSANITY

Within the confines of one's mind
Unending doors are blinding
What is real and what is fake
Confusion I never seem to escape
Continue to walk making no ground
Blissful silence, there is no sound
Hearing what goes in and out
A noise of nowhere comes about
Follow it to a door locked in chain
Open and see person tied up in vain
Dead inside with hollowed eyes
Accepting fate to my surprise
They look up and speak to me with smile
"Locked you are and locked you will stay"
"We have been driven to insanity anyway"
Though confused the door closed
Signal or sign
He too stuck within the confines of his mind

RAIN UNDER SUNSET

Memories stretched across time
Black and white stain my canvas
As happiness drapes in grime
Once here but gone so quickly
Like Sunset under the rain so swiftly
Your back dipped in warmth
Smile as big as mine
Memories bring your death forth
Now your voice passes so quickly
Like sunset under the rain so swiftly
First to teach and offer guidance
First to see
First to cry with me
First to show life's beauty
Smile on face as you sink into sea
Like sunset under the rain so swiftly

QUIVERING FLAME

SET YOUR HEART ON FIRE!
Or so I thought
Death loomed like a lingering thought
Battle night & Day
Couldn't save you from passing away
Always said feed the flame
Your last words bore my shame
Strong-willed the flame in your heart
Put out like flashlights in dark
Will unyielding gave hope
Made our flames stronger than yoke
Legs weak, body shaken
Fought until the last enemy was taken
Eternal darkness seeps your body
And I dare say
How do you feed a quivering flame

PERMISSIVE DISGRACE

Sweet as honey
Soft as silk
Lies bitterness doesn't wilt
Calm as wind
Smooth as paint
Words shape one's fate
Cold like water
Consistent as the tide
Heart has nothing to hide
Sharp as swords
Perfect like a slash
Actions deeper than any gash
Insufferable silence
Please be silenced
Keep feeding this plate
Of Permissive Disgrace

NERVOUS MAZE

Adrenaline pumping in my veins
Nothing has since felt same
Love's essence and shadows gaze
Tripping heart like a minefield maze
To feel proclivity within sadness
Addicted to Madness
Yeah it feels like the very first time
Eyes seep into mine
Scared to let go
Yet easy to show
Fearful addiction or manipulation
Ever nervous situation
Can't tell your shadows from the dark
Light within about to depart
Hurricane within mind
Yet contract signed
Though forced to stay
Shadow begins to say
Follow you forever I'm certain
But I still get nervous

PEACEFUL ABYSS

Lost ground
Made up thoughts
Struggle for life
All to a halt
Love and passion burned within
Put out with a peaceful glimmer
Looking down
Can't see ground
Useless is as useless does
Falls without sound
First ending new beginning
Freedom in menacing pain
Such fate of those who gain
Fleeting feeling in the end
Tenebrosity may rend
This abyss was peaceful in the end

DEAREST UNDERTONE

Start of something new
Expecting more getting Less
Blocked by confusion inside
Simple notions fade to black
Hands crumbled under nothing
Eyes dead to water
Heart turned cold
Warmth no longer sought
Unnoticed almost invisible
Looking through ones own reflections
Pulled deeper into abyss
Yet one can't stand
Under emotions quicksand

UNEXPRESSED SENTENCE

Told to hold high
Though dying inside
Told to stay strong
Though weak I may be
Told to not cry
Though devastated I am
Taught to be brave
Though cowardly I was
Taught to fight
Though my body break easy
Taught to endure
Though can't take it anymore
Told hearts heal
Taught wounds mend
Told broken bones become strong
Taught to stand back up
Though learned, told, and taught
One's always endlessly Distraught

ACCOMPANIED POLTROON

Here or there
One might run everywhere
Feet so fleeting
Eyes never meeting
Head down never seeing
Farther and Farther
Never-ending goal
Impossible to grasp
Breath, slow steady rasp
Strained of Confidence
Like a king taken from his precipice
Those who congratulated
Now speak in silence
Those who smiled
Now smile for eternity
Those wings of guidance
Now fill the air
Yet here to stand to honor the rest
All to do is to keep fleeing into darkness

CLOUDED JUDGMENT

Should I runaway

Or

Am I here to stay

Confusion in mind

But your words so kind

Outwards looking in

Are we the same within

One in mind

And

One in body

Connection feels hazed and sodden

Delusions seep

Fear sets in deep

Fake

Or

Real

Clouded judgement is what I feel

LOVE

Never realized till I had it
Forever taken from me
As I walk aimlessly
Memories think to past lost
Even now that you're gone
Crying inside never stops
But smiles upon your thoughts
You were my mystery
Everything wanted and could be
There when I fell
There when I faltered
Rays to my sunshine
Calm after the storm
Though you are silent
I will scream
My Love

SMILES

Carried yet so far
Even in the state you are
Smiles are everyday
Never deserved it
Should have treasured it
Joy to soft soul
Even one hard as coal
Smiles kept me going
Rain pours
Storms rage
But smiles everyday

NO ONE

Who watched
Who waited
No one
Who listened
Who helped
No one
Who cared
Who shared
Who decided speak
Who decided to take a peek
No one

SHROUD'S INIQUITY

So we run
Taste of light what we crave
Insanity, hunger, death go away
These eyes see enough decay
Losses between distance
Sorrowful cries fill their stiffness
Barren tears become calmness
Crimson fingers hold weight
A void no longer filled with hate
Nothing will satiate
Resist and refrain
Yet temptation seeks gain
Black cloud of sin reaches out
Though good deeds make us shout
Though covered in shame
We have nothing to gain
Scream and shout
Running about
Feet tread upon Fall
Daylight far from we at all

SMOKY LUMINESCENCE

Sparks fly in a haze
Judgment clouds these days
Seeking and finding you will not
Aspiration is but a thought
Color coated eyes brim with delight
But Dull colors are my plight
Lit together into a trance
All around darkness prance
Continuation on and on
Cycle repeat until it's gone
Deafening Resonance all around
Put my ears to ground
Sky fades into Black
Hopeless tears in no lack

REMORSEFUL BLUE YONDER

Once Loved, Flew high
Difference filled with love
Acceptance from one not many
Heart cried because others
Silence grasped ones lips
Told Aberration and Abomination
Pitted into despair
Flight obscured storm
Flashes cause demise
Once again alone in this
Blue Yonder

END UNDERSTANDING

Did you hear it? Did you see It? Did you understand? Were you listening? Letting out failures, disparity, thoughts or judgments, our shortcomings, our iniquities, sins define us. Little do we realize and fail to look around, to see the shadows cast on others that cast on us and little do those who don't have such shadows realize The chaos around silent, yet very loud. We can't let our experiences and our own self-doubts inside us to form who we are in the future. All we can do is push forward out of our own shadows.

www.ingramcontent.com/pod-product-compliance
Lightning Source LLC
Chambersburg PA
CBHW060558030426

42337CB00019B/3568